IF FOUI

M000073501

👤 _____

✉ _____
_____

📱 _____

Greater Than a Tourist Book Series
Reviews from Readers

i

Good information to have to plan my trip to this destination.

-Pennie Farrell, Mexico

Great ideas for a port day.

-Mary Martin USA

Aptly titled, you won't just be a tourist after reading this book. You'll be greater than a tourist!

-Alan Warner, Grand Rapids, USA

Even though I only have three days to spend in San Miguel in an upcoming visit, I will use the author's suggestions to guide some of my time there. An easy read - with chapters named to guide me in directions I want to go.

-Robert Catapano, USA

Great insights from a local perspective! Useful information and a very good value!

-Sarah, USA

This series provides an in-depth experience through the eyes of a local. Reading these series will help you to travel the city in with confidence and it'll make your journey a unique one.

-Andrew Teoh, Ipoh, Malaysia

GREATER THAN A TOURIST- SEVILLE ANDALUSIA SPAIN

50 Travel Tips from a Local

Robin Custers

Cover designed by: Ivana Stamenkovic
Cover Image: https://pixabay.com/en/regional-parliament-spain-andalusia-655015/

CZYK Publishing Since 2011.

Greater Than a Tourist
Visit our website at www.GreaterThanaTourist.com

Lock Haven, PA
All rights reserved.
ISBN: 9781723981654

>TOURIST

50 TRAVEL TIPS FROM A LOCAL

BOOK DESCRIPTION

Are you excited about planning your next trip?

Do you want to try something new?

Would you like some guidance from a local?

If you answered yes to any of these questions, then this Greater Than a Tourist book is for you.

Greater Than a Tourist- Seville Andalusia Spain by Robin Custers offers the inside scoop on Seville. Most travel books tell you how to travel like a tourist. Although there is nothing wrong with that, as part of the Greater Than a Tourist series, this book will give you travel tips from someone who has lived at your next travel destination.

In these pages, you will discover advice that will help you throughout your stay. This book will not tell you exact addresses or store hours but instead will give you excitement and knowledge from a local that you may not find in other smaller print travel books.

Travel like a local. Slow down, stay in one place, and get to know the people and the culture. By the time you finish this book, you will be eager and prepared to travel to your next destination.

TABLE OF CONTENTS

DEDICATION

This book is dedicated to my mother, Karin Sneijder. Thank you for your unbiased support, and for always being there for me, no matter the distance between us.

And to all my friends and family in Seville who made me feel so welcome, helped me whenever I needed help, and taught me how to be a true Sevillana.

ABOUT THE AUTHOR

Robin Custers, a small-town girl from The Netherlands who never thought she could live in a big city, lost her heart to a beautiful city in the south of Spain. On a warm spring evening in June 2016, she first set foot in Seville and it was love at first sight. After this first trip, she travelled to Seville repeatedly until she eventually moved there in January of 2018. She earned her Associate's Degree in Tourism Management that same year and started working for a Spanish - Dutch bike tour company, as a tour guide in the city with the largest historical center in Europe.

Besides her work, she loves to sing. She is also an aspiring photographer, and loves travelling to discover new places and expand her horizon.

HOW TO USE THIS BOOK

The Greater Than a Tourist book series was written by someone who has lived in an area for over three months. The goal of this book is to help travelers either dream or experience different locations by providing opinions from a local. The author has made suggestions based on their own experiences. Please do your own research before traveling to the area in case the suggested places are unavailable.

FROM THE PUBLISHER

Traveling can be one of the most important parts of a person's life. The anticipation and memories that you have are some of the best. As a publisher of the Greater Than a Tourist book series, as well as the popular 50 Things to Know book series, we strive to help you learn about new places, spark your imagination, and inspire you. Wherever you are and whatever you do I wish you safe, fun, and inspiring travel.

Lisa Rusczyk Ed. D.
CZYK Publishing

OUR STORY

Traveling is a passion of the "Greater than a Tourist" series creator. Lisa studied abroad in college, and for their honeymoon Lisa and her husband toured Europe. During her travels to Malta, an older man tried to give her some advice based on his own experience living on the island since he was a young boy. She was not sure if she should talk to the stranger but was interested in his advice. When traveling to some places she was wary to talk to locals because she was afraid that they weren't being genuine. Through her travels, Lisa learned how much locals had to share with tourists. Lisa created the "Greater Than a Tourist" book series to help connect people with locals. A topic that locals are very passionate about sharing.

WELCOME TO
> TOURIST

INTRODUCTION

"The world is a book, and those who do not travel read only one page"

– Saint Augustine

When we travel, it's most comfortable to go with the masses, and stick to what we know. But nothing enriches your travel experience more than stepping out of your bubble. They say the best things in life are just outside your comfort zone. I can say, from personal experience, this is true.

When I came to Seville for the first time, I was immediately captivated by the beauty of this city. I grew up in a small town in the south of the Netherlands. Horse riding was my sport and I was so used to being out in the countryside that I told myself (and everyone around me) that I would never live in a big city. And then I went to Seville.

There is something about this city that just reels you in. The beautiful architecture, the endless stories behind every stone in every building, but most of all, the people who live here and their culture. I'm a tour guide, so I meet a lot of new people from many different countries every single day. These people are usually in Seville for the first time and will only be there a couple of days. All these people always tell me one thing at the end of our tours: "There is so much to see here, we have to come back!"

Sevillians say: "Sevilla tiene un color especial" ("Seville has a special color") and it is most certainly true. This special color is Seville's superpower that makes you want to come back for more. Make your trip to Seville one filled with memorable experiences, and one you'll never forget, and I hope that with the help of these tips Seville works its magic on you too.

1. HOW TO GREET

When you are in a new place with a culture that is unfamiliar to you, it can be a bit daunting to communicate with the inhabitants of that place. Books can only tell you so much, and there is no one better than these inhabitants to tell you all about the place they call home. But greetings in Spain can be quite complicated, as there are different 'rules', depending on your gender or status.

When a woman greets another person, male or female, they usually do so by exchanging two kisses, one on each cheek. When two men greet each other, they usually shake hands or hug. Sometimes they also exchange two kisses on the cheeks, but only if they know each other well. In Spain, this is not seen as gay. If you're not sure what to do, a simple handshake will always do the trick.

When greeting someone for the first time, it is polite to say your name. If you want to say: "Hello, I'm – *your name* –, nice to meet you!" in Spanish, you can say the following; if you're a man, you say: "Hola, soy – *your name* –, encanta**do** de conocerse." If you're a woman, you say: "Hola, soy – *your name* –, encanta**da** de conocerse."

15

2. BRUSH UP ON YOUR SPANISH

Spanish people often appreciate it if you (at least attempt to) communicate with them in their own language. Most people in Spain do not speak any other languages. They translate everything to Spanish, they voice-over every movie or tv show and most Spaniards never had an English class at school. Understandable, because why would they? Spanish is one of the most-spoken languages in the world. Therefore, it would be a good idea to learn some useful Spanish phrases. If you speak Spanish to the locals, it shows them that you're willing to make an effort and they will be flattered.

A good idea is to bring a small Spanish dictionary with you wherever you go, so you can find the words you need in any situation. However, nowadays everyone has easy access to the internet through their smartphones, so an online translator can also do the trick. Don't translate whole sentences at once though, for the translating machines are not the best at correct grammar and might give a completely different meaning to what you're trying to say.

3. BEST TIME TO TRAVEL

The best time to travel to Seville is, in contrary to popular belief, in the spring and autumn. I would try to avoid Sevilla in the hot summer months, especially July and August. During these months, temperatures can reach up to 120°F! This is one of the main reasons why the siesta is still a big thing in the south of Spain. Most people who live in the city escape the heat for a few weeks and go to the coast, so in summer the city is quite empty and 'abandoned'.

Seville is the most beautiful in spring and autumn. The temperatures are pleasant, it's not too hot and not too cold. The inhabitants are all in the city, bars are open until late and shops are open all day.

4. SUMMER HEAT

Seville is also known as 'the oven of Europe' and 'the frying pan of Spain', because of the scorching heat during the summer months. With temperatures regularly surpassing 100°F, most locals escape try to escape the heat as much as possible. They do this either by going to the coast for a few weeks or staying indoors during the hottest hours of the day.

When you're in the city in August, try to plan most of your outdoor-activities in the morning, before 1:00 or 2:00 PM. The temperature reaches its maximum between 5:00 and 8:00 PM, after that the sun goes down and so does the temperature. Try to avoid direct sunlight as much as possible and go out well-prepared.

One of the most important things is to stay hydrated. Make sure that you always have a bottle of water with you when you venture out into the streets. You can also buy water on every street corner, so don't worry if you don't have any beforehand. Wear loose, lightweight clothing and slap on that SPF! The sun is so strong in Seville that you can even get a sunburn in the shade. Don't forget to apply SPF regularly throughout the day, so you're always protected.

But even after taking all the precautions mentioned, you can easily overheat if you're too active without allowing your body the time to get acclimated. Do not jump out of the plane and on to a bicycle to ride around the city for hours during a hot afternoon but take it easy for at least one day before exercising. This way you will be better conditioned to survive the extreme summer heat.

5. SAFETY: BE SMART

Seville is one of the safest cities I have ever been to, and as a young woman, I am perfectly comfortable walking around the city by myself both day and night. However, just as in any other place in the world, you still have to be smart. Don't walk in the lonely dark alleys at 2AM, don't leave your bag open and don't carry your wallet or phone around in your back pocket. I would also advise against venturing too far outside the city center. There is not much to see there, and the slightly higher risk of becoming a victim of theft is not worth it. In short, don't make yourself an easy target for those who do have bad intentions. As long as you use your common sense, you will be fine.

6. GYPSIES: DON'T FALL FOR THE TRAPS

You will see them at every tourist attraction, offering rosemary to every tourist they see. The mistake that some tourists make, is accepting the rosemary and taking it from them, unaware of the fact that they are not handing out rosemary for free. Once you touch the rosemary, they will not let go of your hand until you pay for it. Sometimes, they will tell your fortune and ask for 20 Euros in return.

When offered some rosemary or fortune telling, try to keep your distance, give them a friendly nod and a "no, gracias", and just keep walking.

7. AVOID LONG LINES

If you want to visit Seville's Cathedral that opens at 11AM, and want to avoid long lines, your first thought will probably be: "I will make sure that I am there at 10:50AM, so I will be one of the first people there and it won't be so busy yet." In the past that may have been the case, but nowadays, people start lining up outside the Cathedral at 10:30AM.

My advice is that if you want to visit any tourist attraction in Spain where you must wait in line, go during the siesta time. This is usually between 1PM and 4/5PM. During this time, most Spanish visitors will be having their lunch and their siesta, so they won't be waiting in line, and the wait times will be a lot shorter.

8. WHAT TO WEAR

Spanish people usually dress a bit more conservative. Spanish women look very put together. Especially when going out, they wear fancy outfits which are not too revealing. Knee length skirts, tops with a high neckline or blouses and big earrings. You'll also see a lot of bright colors in Seville. Usually a bright colored top is paired with black pants or jeans, or the other way around. Color-coordination is very important. If you wear a dress with pink and green in it, you wear matching accessories.

Spanish women almost always wear heels, and since most people choose walking over any other form of transportation, they walk miles and miles in them. I have always envied women here, and wished I had their heel-walking skills. It's almost like they were born in them!

9. PASSIONATE IN CONVERSATION, ARE THEY HAPPY OR ANGRY?

When you think of the stereotypical Spaniard, one of the first characteristics that comes to mind is 'passionate'. And passionate they definitely are. Especially in conversation. So passionate that sometimes, to foreigners, it might seem that they are having a heated argument about a very serious matter, while they are just discussing the weather and what they are going to have for lunch that day.

Don't be intimidated if a Spaniard sits or stands close to you while talking, makes direct eye contact most of the time and touches you on the shoulder every now and then.

10. WORLD'S MOST BEAUTIFUL ROYAL PALACE

The Real Alcazar of Seville is my absolute favorite place in the city. This beautiful historical palace was built by the Moors that ruled the south of Spain from the 8th until the end of the 15th century and expanded by the many Spanish kings and queens that lived there. It was declared a World Heritage Site by UNESCO in 1987. Each room inside the palace has its own rich history. For example, the Sala de Audiencias is the room where Columbus requested permission and funds to explore the world for Spain from Queen Isabella I in 1492, and it is said that Amerigo Vespucci prepared his first travels to the continent that was named after him, America, in the Cuarto del Almirante. Be sure to read every sign in every room, so you know what happened in every room of the palace.

11. HANG OUT WITH LOCALS IN ALAMEDA DE HÉRCULES

This long square is worth checking out if you are looking for a good place to eat where not many tourists go. You can recognize this square by four pillars, two at each end. The oldest two pillars come from an ancient Roman temple that was located in Calle Mármoles. This temple had six columns. In the 16th century, locals wanted to move four of these columns to Alameda de Hercules. The first two columns were moved successfully, but unfortunately the third one did not survive the journey. They left the last three columns of the Roman temple in place (which you can still see in Calle Mármoles today) and reconstructed two columns to place them in Alameda de Hercules.

Until the World Expo of 1992, this square was the of sex, drugs and rock 'n roll, and most visitors would avoid embodiment this place. To fight the prostitution and drug problem in this square, they started by building a big police station right in the middle. This made the square more family-friendly and has turned it into a place where locals get together and hang out.

On this square, you will find all kinds of restaurants. From the typical Spanish tapas bars, to Japanese sushi and vegan restaurants. La Alameda is also a popular place to go out at night. Almost every bar is filled to the brim, after the sun goes down until the sun comes up. If you're looking for a good place to have a fun night out with your friends and meet new people, Alameda de Hercules is where you should go.

12. ROYAL HOUSES YOU CAN VISIT

There are still a few grand houses/palaces that belonged to, or still belong to, royal families and that are open to visitors. These houses and their long history show the wealth of the families who lived there (and still live there) and their transformation throughout the centuries.

The Palacio de las Dueñas is a centuries old palace in the center of Seville. It has been the home of the Dukes and Duchesses of Alba for over 450 years. The late Duchess Cayetana of Alba had a passion for bullfighting, flamenco and art. This is what you see all around you when you visit this palace. Her personality is present in every single room. Some of here noteworthy guests at this palace were Jacqueline Kennedy, Wallis Simpson, Grace Kelly and Salvador

Dalí. Palacio de las Dueñas is not a typical royal palace, but definitely worth a visit.

The Palacio de la Condesa de Lebrija is one of the most beautiful and most expensive houses in Seville. It is located right in the city center, close to the shopping streets and the Metropol Parasol. The Countess of Lebrija bought this 16th century house in 1901, and it now houses her valuable collection of historic artifacts and art pieces. She had a great collection of Roman mosaics and sculptures, and paintings by Dutch, Flemish and Spanish renaissance and baroque masters. You can explore the ground floor on your own. If you want to visit the top floor, you must go on a guided tour. I would recommend doing so, because here you will find the rooms left exactly as the Countess' family lived in them.

Last, but not least, is the Casa de Pilatos. This is the home of the Dukes and Duchesses of Medinaceli. This palace is over 500 years old and has one of the largest *azulejo* (typical Spanish and Portuguese decorated ceramic tiles) collections in the world. If you've seen the films Kingdom of Heaven (2005) or Knight and Day (2010), this palace might look familiar to you, as a few scenes from these movies were filmed in this palace.

13. SHOPPING: WHERE TO GO

Seville has three big shopping streets in the center. The biggest of the three is Calle Tetuan. Here you will find all the big international brands that you really can find anywhere in the world. Stores like Zara, Adidas, Sephora, you name it. There are two smaller shopping streets that run parallel to Calle Tetuan. They are called Calle Sierpes and Calle Cuna. These are the older, more traditional shopping streets. Here you will find, for example, the abanicos (hand fans), flamenco dresses and traditional communion clothing. If you are looking for the typical Spanish shops, I'd recommend going here. However, in Calle Sierpes and Calle Cuna you will often find that most shops are closed during the siesta time. This is usually between 2PM and 5PM. Shops in Seville usually open from 10AM and 10PM, so if you plan on going shopping, do it around the siesta time so you won't be disappointed by closed doors.

There are also a few shopping malls, these are outside the center. Nervion (close to the Sevilla F.C. soccer stadium) and Los Arcos are the two bigger malls where you'll find most popular brands. There are also a few outlet centers, where you'll find products from expensive brands for discounted prices. The ones closest to Seville are Sevilla Fashion Outlet (close to Seville Airport) and Sevilla Factory (in adjacent town Dos Hermanas).

14. EXPO OF 1929

Seville had two large expositions in the past 100 years. The first one was the Ibero-American Exposition in 1929. This fair was held to improve trade relationships between Spain, Portugal and North and South America. It also took place in the same year as the crash on Wall Street, so it didn't have a big effect on the trade relationships, but it did have a major effect on the city's 'look'. A total of 117 buildings were built in the years leading up to the Expo, of which 25 can still be found in the city today. The most famous constructions built especially for this Expo were Plaza de España and the Alfonso XIII hotel. Most of the pavilions built for this Expo now have a different use, for example the Plaza de España now houses several government offices, the old casino has now turned into the Lope de Vega theatre and pavilions of other countries have turned into museums or consulates. Most of these buildings can be found in and around the Maria Luisa park.

15. EXPO OF 1992

Seville's first expo took place in 1929, but if you turn the last two numbers around, in 1992, Seville held the World Expo. The theme of this exposition was 'The Era of Discoveries', for it was held exactly 500 years after Cristopher Columbus set sail from Spain and discovered the Americas. The pavilions were built on Isla Cartuja, surrounding the Cartuja Monastery where Columbus prepared for his first voyage to the New World. This monastery is still there today, along with some of the pavilions of the World Expo. Isla Cartuja is now divided into two halves, one half has become an office zone or so-called research and development park, and the other half has become a theme park called Isla Mágica.

The area feels a bit 'abandoned' now, as it's not how it was before. Most of the pavilions have disappeared or have turned in to offices. But if you are traveling to Seville with kids, Isla Mágica might be a fun day out. Especially during the summertime, as Isla Mágica also has a water park called Agua Mágica where your kids can enjoy themselves and cool off on a hot summer's day.

16. HOTEL ALFONSO XIII: NO ROOM NEEDED

Hotel Alfonso XIII was built for the Expo of 1929. It was named after the King of Spain at the time, and it was a place where the important guests of the Ibero-American Expo could spend the night. So, it was built as a luxurious hotel, and it has always been a luxurious hotel. The hotel now has 5 stars, and it is one of the most luxurious hotels in the city. Every time celebrities are in the city, 9 out of 10 times they stay in this hotel. For example, the Game of Thrones cast, Tom Cruise and Cameron Diaz all stayed in this hotel while they were working in Seville. Safe to say, this hotel is the most famous hotel in the city, and with that also comes a pretty steep price.

But what most people do not know is that you can go inside the hotel, even if you don't have a room there. You can visit the most luxurious bathroom in the entire city for free! But you must be careful if you sit down anywhere (well, not if you sit down on the toilet, but you know what I mean), a waiter may approach you and ask you if you want anything to drink. If you've been to any northern European city before, the prices seem reasonable. You'll pay around €5 for a coffee, maybe €6/€7 for a glass of wine. This is a lot more expensive than the €1,50 coffee you can get in most bars on the streets in Spain, but at least you'll be drinking your coffee in the fancy Alfonso XIII hotel.

17. CROSS THE RIVER – GO TO TRIANA

When visiting Seville, most people don't cross the Guadalquivir river to go to Triana, and just stay in the city center. But this district has so much character and such a rich history, it is definitely worth a visit.

In the past, Triana was the poor part of town where sailors, workers and gypsies lived. Over the years it has turned into the place where everyone wants to be, and everyone wants to live. It is the birthplace of many famous bullfighters, and it is also said to be the birthplace of the flamenco.

If you were to ask the people who live there where they are from, they would tell you they are from Triana, not Seville. They are *Trianeros*, not *Sevillianos*. Crossing the bridge to go to the center is "going to Seville", even though Triana is just a district of Seville.

On 'the other side' of the Isabel II Bridge (known as the Triana Bridge) in Triana, you will find the Mercado de Triana. This traditional market only opens in the morning, and this is where locals go to buy all their fresh foods. Inside the building, you will find remains of the Castle of San Jorge, a medieval fortress where many people were tortured and held captive during the Spanish Inquisition. There is a museum on the Inquisition inside the ruins, right next door to the food market.

18. THE BEST FLAMENCO

Because Triana is known as the birthplace of flamenco, it is also said to be the place to see the best flamenco in the city. The best flamenco shows are the ones that happen spontaneously in one of the many bars in Triana. The problem with these spontaneous shows is in the meaning of the word spontaneous; they are never announced. They usually happen late at night and in random places, so you just have to be lucky that you're in the right place at the right time

If you really want to see flamenco, but don't have the time to sit in random bars in Triana every night, I suggest going to a *tablao*. These are the typical flamenco theaters, and there are several in the city center. Ticket prices for good flamenco shows of 1,5 hours range from €35 to €45. Some places also sell tickets including tapas, but I'd advise against getting those. You get little time to finish your food, and when you're so mesmerized by the flamenco show that you forget you have food in front of you, your food will be cold by the end of the show and you have to leave without eating anything. Just go to a tapas bar before or after the show, and just get the normal flamenco tickets.

Be sure to make a reservation for a flamenco show, if you are planning on going to see one. When there are a lot of people in the city, the good shows will be fully booked days before. To avoid disappointment at the door, call the tablao beforehand to reserve your seats.

19. AZULEJOS: THE CERAMIC SHOPS

Most of the azulejos, the beautiful ceramic tile-work, you see in the city comes from Triana. In the past there were many ceramic factories, but the last one closed in 2012 due to the financial crisis in Spain. However, there still are many ceramics shops. I recommend visiting Ceramica Santa Ana, which has a beautiful collection of handmade ceramics and it also has an old factory right next door where you can see how these factories worked and how the ceramic tiles are made.

You can find ceramic shops in the city center as well, but in Triana the prices are a little lower than in the center. So, if you want to score a typical Sevillian souvenir, visit the ceramic shops in Triana.

20. MOST IMPORTANT HOLIDAYS

There are many holidays throughout the year in Seville. Two of the most important celebrations are the Semana Santa and the Feria de Abril. Aside from these two, there are a few big ones which are also celebrated on the streets.

Every year on the 30th of May, it's the day of San Fernando. The holy king Fernando III was the catholic king who conquered Seville from the Moors in 1248. He is the man who brought Catholicism to the city, and since the south of Spain still is very catholic, this king is celebrated every year. On this day, his grave in the Virgen de los Reyes chapel inside the Cathedral opens, and visitors can see his mummified corpse. A somewhat dark tradition, but very interesting to say the least.

The day of Virgen de los Reyes on the 15th of August is the day of the patron saint of Seville. On this day, her statue leaves the Cathedral and goes through the streets in a large procession.

A similar celebration is the day of Santa Ana, which takes place each year on the 26th of July. Santa Ana is the patron saint of Triana, the district on 'the other side of the river', and on this day she goes through the district in a large procession, starting and ending at the Santa Ana church. They say that if you kiss Santa Ana's statue, you have one year of good luck! So, if you're in the city any one of these days, you can be witness to some of Seville's oldest traditions.

21. SEMANA SANTA – SEVILLE'S HOLY WEEK

The Semana Santa, the Holy Week, is the week before Easter and it is the most important religious celebration of the year. During this week, there are multiple processions going through the streets of the city every day, with statues representing the different scenes from the Passion of Jesus Christ, and Holy Virgins. These statues are called *pasos*, most of them are over 300 years old, and they are carried by around 25 to 40 local members of the brotherhood (*hermandad*) of the church where the statue comes from. Each procession has one *paso*, followed by hundreds, and sometimes thousands of *nazarenos*, which are dressed in a very controversial gown. Their outfits look quite similar to those of the K.K.K., but do not worry, the two traditions have nothing in common. They wear the high hats to be closer to the sky and closer to God, while their entire body is covered. They only have two holes for their eyes, so they can be completely anonymous. They walk the procession to repent their sins, to 'suffer' for their beliefs. Some of them even walk the sometimes 12-hour long processions barefoot!

Semana Santa is the busiest week of the year and attracts thousands of visitors every year. If you visit Seville during this week, keep in mind that most of the shops and touristic attractions will be closed and restaurants will usually have a special Semana Santa-menu to better suit the crowds.

22. FERIA DE ABRIL – THE APRIL FAIR

The Feria de Abril – the April Fair – is the most iconic traditional festival in Seville. It takes place two weeks after the Semana Santa on the designated Feria-terrain called the "Real de la Feria", in the district of Los Remedios. This terrain is completely empty most of the year, but during the Feria this terrain is filled with more than a thousand *casetas* (small party tents) and a fair which is called "Calle de Infierno" ("Hell Street"). Each caseta has its own catering service and most of them are private, so they are owned by families, companies or associations. This means that you enter these casetas, unless you know someone inside and they invite you in. If you know a local, you can go to the Feria with them and they can take you to their caseta. Don't worry, if you don't know anyone there you can still enter the few public casetas.

Seville's first Feria de Abril was in the year 1847, and it's one of the most traditional ferias in Spain. The Feria started as a stock market, but has now turned into a week of drinking, dancing and socializing. The party goes on all night, and all morning too! Most people arrive at around 1PM, just before lunch time, and most of them stay until the early hours of the next morning, sometimes even until 9AM!

At the Feria you will only hear one type of music, *the Sevillanas*. This is the typical folk music genre that originated in Seville and it has its own dance. Every local has been dancing this typical dance since before they learned how to walk. It is a more simplified version of the flamenco, and it has a set choreography. Don't be afraid to start dancing with the locals, and don't worry if you don't know the steps yet. Locals will teach you, and your feria will automatically become ten times better!

23. THE FLAMENCO DRESS

One of the most typical aspects of the Feria, aside from all the horses on the streets, is the flamenco dress. A common misconception is that Sevillian women wear this dress all year round, but this dress is only worn during the Feria de Abril.

The flamenco dress has been fashionable since the Ibero-American exposition in Seville in 1929, when high-society women wore these dresses after seeing them on gypsy women. These so-called 'Gitanas' made their own dresses out of old fabric, sewn into nice ruffles at the ankles and wrists to give it a more festive appearance. They are tight-fitting until right above the knee, where they flare out. This makes the dresses hard to walk in, let alone dance in. Therefore, the professional flamenco dancers wear a different style dress that flares out at the waist, so it allows them to move freely.

The average Sevillian woman has 3-4 flamenco dresses. These dresses are the only type of traditional clothing that is still fashionable, and at the same time fashion-sensitive. Every year has a different fashion trend. You often see this difference in the length of the sleeves and skirt, and the size of the ruffles. These dresses are not cheap. Prices range from €250 up to €2.000 and higher. Only women who want to be fashionable buy a new dress every year, but not every woman does this. Most women buy their dresses in the classic style, that stays fashionable every year.

The dress is always paired with a scarf (a *mantoncillo*), a flower in your hair and some big colorful earrings. The craziest color combinations are acceptable. This is also what makes it a very colorful festival.

If you want to wear a flamenco dress to the Feria, but do not want to spend a lot of money on one, you can rent a dress as well. Don't buy the cheaper ones they sell at the souvenir stands, those are dead giveaways that you are a tourist, as they are not the real thing.

Women do not wear their flamenco dress to the Feria every day. The dress-code for the Feria is: flamenco dress, or formal wear. So, if you plan on visiting the feria but don't want to spend money on a dress, just wear something formal and you won't stand out.

A big no-no is wearing a flower in your hair when you're not wearing a flamenco dress. I see a lot of tourists do this, but this, again, is a dead giveaway that you are a tourist. Try to avoid wearing a flower in your hair if you are not wearing a flamenco dress.

24. RESTAURANTS: WHAT TO ORDER

Spain is the country of tapas, with Seville as its culinary capital. There are many restaurants in the city (1 for every 5 inhabitants!) and there is a lot to choose from on the menus. Some typical Sevillian foods that you simply must try during your stay in the city are the pescaito frito (fried fish), serranito (the city's signature sandwich) and my personal favorite, solomillo al whiskey.

Seville is known for its amazing seafood. Fried fish is especially good in this city. *Adobo* is a typical dish, and perhaps one of the most popular. It is dogfish, marinated in a mixture of sherry vinegar, garlic, paprika and more. It has a very strong (and delicious) scent, which lures you into the bars. If you're ever in Calle Tetuan, and you are wondering where the delicious adobo scent comes from, it's Bodeguita Blanco Cerrillo. Their adobo is one of the best in the city, so if you're planning on trying adobo, go there.

25. LA CUENTA, POR FAVOR

When you are in a restaurant in Spain, the communication might prove a little difficult sometimes. Most waiters in the non-touristic restaurants don't know a word of English. That's why it is very useful to know a few key phrases in Spanish to make your breakfast, lunch or dinner in a Spanish restaurant a lot easier.

- "Quería un cafe, por favor" = I would like a coffee, please.
- "¿Tienen comida sin gluten?" = Do you have gluten-free plates?
- "La cuenta, por favor" = The bill, please.
- "Está buenisima!" = It's amazing!
- "¿Qué me recomienda?" = What do you recommend?

If you're not sure what to order, you can ask for the waiter's recommendation and he will probably offer you the restaurant's specialty!

26. BREAKFAST

In Spain, meal times are a lot different from those in other countries. That is why it is good to know at what times Spanish people eat, so you know at around what time you can expect to eat the following meals.

Your breakfast depends on what you have to do in the morning. People who have to get up early for work have breakfast early, but this is usually something simple. A cup of coffee and a piece of fruit or maybe some cereal.

The real breakfast time is at around 10-11AM. This breakfast is a bit more elaborate. Orange juice, coffee, toast with jamón, tomato and olive oil, sometimes even some churros with chocolate. You can order a breakfast like this in most restaurants until noon. After this hour, most restaurants switch to the lunch menu.

27. LUNCH

Instead of dinner, lunch is the largest meal of the day in Spain. Lunchtime is anywhere between 1PM and 4-5PM. It usually has several courses. You have

43

your fish, meat, maybe a salad and afterwards you can have a dessert or some fruit.

When you're on vacation in Spain, it is best to adapt to their meal times. Most shops and businesses are closed during these times, so there won't be much else to do than trying everything Spanish cuisine has to offer. And when that after-lunch-fatigue hits, the siesta time is a perfect excuse to take a quick nap!

28. MERIENDA

Since there is a pretty big gap between lunch and dinner, the Spanish have their merienda, also known as tea-time, right in the middle. This is between 6-8PM. The merienda is usually a cup of coffee or tea, sometimes accompanied by something sweet, such as a cookie or a piece of cake.

This is usually the time when most tourists are looking for a place to have dinner, and the only places they find that are opened at this hour are the *cafeterias*. They open only for breakfast and merienda, and they usually don't serve warm meals. Therefore, it's best to adapt to the Spanish rhythm and have your dinner before or after the merienda time.

29. DINNER

Dinnertime in Spain is between 10PM and midnight, and it's not what you might be used to. Spanish dinner is a smaller version of the lunch. It is also a warm meal, but a bit less elaborate. When people eat at home, it is usually something simple. An omelet, some vegetables or a small sandwich. When they eat in a bar, they usually take one or two tapas and that's it.

Most bars and restaurants open for dinner at around 8PM and close at midnight. This is also the time when you will see most people on the streets, as shops close at 10PM. So, make good use of your siesta time, so you can enjoy the city until long after the sun goes down!

30. GO FOR THE LEAST ATTRACTIVE BARS

Since there are so many restaurants in the city, it might be difficult to spot the good ones. If you want to find the typical Spanish tapas bars where locals go, try not to fall for the typical tourist traps. These so-called tourist traps are restaurants that might look nice, calm and clean, but they serve their food in smaller portions, are not always that good and they make you pay way more than what you might pay in a normal tapas bar. How can you spot these tourist traps? Look at the menus outside before entering a restaurant. If they charge €3,50 for a beer, there is a 90% chance that you will be overpaying in this restaurant.

What I'm going to say now might sound very contradictory, but if you want to eat what locals eat for the best price possible, this is what you must do; you must look for bars that look the least attractive. Bright lights, napkins on the floor, filled with locals. Those are the bars with the good food and good prices.

31. EAT OUTSIDE THE CENTER

If you get the chance, try to go to the bars just outside the city center. Often the tapas bars and restaurants in the middle of the city center know that they are right where all the tourists are, and they thus are a bit more expensive than the ones that are outside the touristic area. The Macarena district is a good area to go to, because it's on the other side of the center from where the Cathedral and Royal Palace are. If you look at the map of Seville, you'll see one main road going around the center. Cross that road, and you get to the neighborhoods where little tourists go. That's where you will find the cheaper but great tapas bars where locals go. If you want to eat a lot, for a good price, go to La Cigala de Oro. Another one of my favorites is La Taurina, a restaurant completely in bullfighting theme. Even their delicious serranitos have bullfighting themed names!

32. GO TO THE FERIA MARKET

The historical Lonja de Feria is a fresh food market by morning, and by night it turns into an amazing place to hang out and try all different kinds of (also non-Spanish) food. In the various tapas stalls you can order whatever you like. Some say their *paella* is one of the best in the city. But they do not only offer the typical Spanish dishes. If you've already spent a few days in Spain and you've had enough jamón and fried fish to last you a few years, you'll find just what you need here. The Mexican and Japanese cuisine can also be found here, among others.

The idea is that you buy a ticket for around €4, and you can exchange that ticket for a drink and a tapa at a stall of your choice. Aside from these tapas stalls, there are also a few separate tapas bars inside the building which offer all different types of dishes.

33. BEST TAPAS STREETS

If you don't feel like venturing too far out of the city center, there are a few streets I can recommend where you are guaranteed to have a good meal (if you know what to look for of course, see tip number 30).

The most popular street is Calle Mateos Gago. This street starts right across form the Giralda Tower of the Cathedral, and it has both tapas bars and bigger restaurants. Here you must be careful about the before mentioned tourist traps, because this is also where a lot of tourists go.

On the other side of the Cathedral, your best bet is going to Calle Adriano and the adjacent Calle Arfe. And while you're there, go into the little alleyways as well. This area is packed with good tapas bars, and there is something for everyone.

If you want a meal with a nice view of the river, go to Calle Betis. This is one of the most iconic streets in the city, and it runs alongside the river in the Triana district. In the morning there is not much to do there, as most of the bars are still closed. But go there after noon, and most bars will have opened and set up their terraces on the other side of the street, from where you can see the water, the bullfighting arena, the old Moorish tower named the Torre del Oro and the oldest bridge in the city, the Isabel II Bridge.

34. GOING OUT AT NIGHT

As you may know, the Spanish lifestyle is more laid-back, everything moves as a slower pace and their nights seem longer than nights in any other country. Especially in the summertime, when people stay indoors most of the day and only come out when the sun goes down. When going out at night, most Spaniards don't leave their house until after 11PM, and don't come home until 5 or 6AM.

If you just want to hang out and drink some cocktails, there are plenty of bars to suit your needs. A typical and very diverse local hangout spot is La Alameda de Hércules, so if you go there you'll be sure to find something. You can also go to Kiosko Bombay or Muelle New York for some delicious cocktails and good music by the riverside. Where Calle Adriano meets Paseo de Cristóbal Colon you'll find several bars and clubs that are always buzzing with people.

There are also many clubs, if you're just looking for a place to dance the night away. The best clubs can be found on Plaza de Armas and Isla Cartuja. Most people go there after 2AM, and don't leave until the early hours of the morning. There are also a few

open-air clubs close to the Maria Luisa Park, but most
of them are only open during the summer months.

35. WALKING IN SEVILLE

Seville's center is relatively small, compared to
other cities. You can walk from one side of the center
to the other in less than 35 minutes. Most locals
choose walking as their way of getting around,
because you can take the shortest routes through the
small streets without having to worry about traffic
and one-way streets. This is also the perfect way to
take everything in and see the whole city. As Seville
has the largest historic city center in Europe, there is
something to see around every corner.

36. BICYCLE PATHS

When walking in the city, be careful about bicycle
paths, as they are not always very noticeable.
Especially on the big street in the city center, Avenida
de la Constitución, the bicycle paths are pretty much
invisible at first sight, and you'll probably realize

51

they are there after you've already had 5 angry cyclists telling you to get out of the way.

Cycling is new to Seville, and the roads in the center were not designed to have bicycle paths. Therefore, the paths that exist today were improvised, and do not always make sense. In most streets, the bicycle paths have a bright green color. Except for the ones in the center around the Cathedral. Those can be recognized by silver 'buttons' on the road, which have bicycles on them.

37. EXPLORE THE CITY BY BIKE

Did you know that Seville is one of the best bike cities in the world? The city is very flat, compared to other cities in the south of Spain, and many locals happily use its 100 miles of cycle lanes daily. I always recommend this to anyone travelling to the city, but especially to those who want to see as much as they can in a short time.

If you don't have much time in the city but you do want to see as much as possible, rent a bike somewhere. There are several companies in the cities where you can rent bikes. Some of them also organize bike tours, like Andalucía Tours & Discovery. They organize tours inside and outside the city, in several languages and have great quality bikes (with gears and suspension, because you'd want to be comfortable while exploring the city).

Do a bike tour on your first day in Seville. This way you'll see a lot of the city in only a short time and get an idea of which places you want to spend the rest of your time in Seville visiting. When it's hot out, which it is a lot in Seville, going on a bike tour in the morning will be more doable than walking around in the city center. Riding the bike gives you a nice fresh breeze, while moving through the city at a fast pace and learning a lot of new information while you do so.

38. TAXIS IN SEVILLA

Taxis are a good way to get around in Seville, because you can hop on anywhere and they will drop you off right where you tell them to (like every taxi in the world, really). The Sevillian taxis are white, and have a yellow line on the side, and you see them everywhere you go. Taxis are convenient when you're in the center (where almost no buses go) and you don't feel like walking all the way back to your hotel.

You'll always find a few lined up on the side of the Cathedral in Calle Alemanes, next to Plaza de España and next to Metropol Parasol. Those are a few spots where you'll always find taxis, but if they are too far away, you can always wave one down anywhere in the city.

39. TAKING THE BONOBUS

If you're planning on traveling by bus a lot in Seville, it might be a good idea to buy a Bonobus pass. This is a rechargeable pass that you can use on the buses and on trams in Seville. If you buy a ticket on the bus, it will cost you €1,40 (which is cheap as it is). If you use your Bonobus pass, you'll only pay around €0,70 per bus ride. And it doesn't matter how long you stay on the bus. You don't have to check in and check out again when you leave. You only check in, and then you can stay on the bus – or tram – for as long as you want, since you paid already.

40. BEST WAY TO TRAVEL TO & FROM THE AIRPORT

The most convenient way would be to travel by taxi. They usually have a set price of around €35, and they will take you from the airport to your hotel. This is not always the case, so just to be sure, ask before you get in the taxi what the eventual price will be. Even though this is more convenient, it is way more expensive than taking the airport shuttle bus for €4.

In 35 minutes, this bus drives from the airport to the other side of the city center, while stopping at several bus stops on the way. It leaves every 25-30, from 5AM until 1AM the next day.

Most people don't know this shuttle bus exists, but now you do, so I'd suggest taking the bus from the airport to the center and spending the money you saved on a taxi fare in a typical Spanish tapas bar instead!

41. BEST PLACES TO STAY

When you're looking for a place to stay in Seville, it's best to stay in – or close to – the center. Planning on traveling to Seville in the summer? Choose a hotel with a swimming pool. Since there are not so many public swimming pools in the city and Seville doesn't have a beach, having one at your hotel is a must.

There are many hotels in the city, but there are a few with a historical backstory. For example, the Alfonso XIII was built for the Ibero-American Expo in 1929, and it is by far one of the most beautiful hotels in the city. It is a bit expensive however, but if you can afford it I would go there.

Another interesting hotel is hotel Las Casas de la Judería. This is also referred to as 'a city within the city', because it is made up out of 27 different houses, all of them historical houses from the old Jewish quarter, Barrio Santa Cruz. Some of these houses were palaces and others were common houses, so each room looks completely different. If you're a sucker for historical buildings and interesting stories, you might find this hotel very interesting.

42. SEVILLE BEACH, IS THAT A THING?

Unfortunately, no. Seville Beach is not a thing. As you may know, Seville is in the center of Andalusia, far away from the coast line. The nearest beach is about a 1,5-hour drive away from the city, and it is forbidden to swim in the Guadalquivir river as well. Seville is also the hottest city in Europe, so the fact that is has no beach can be quite an inconvenience. There are a few public pools in the city you can go to, some of them are aquatic parks. One I mentioned before is Agua Mágica, on the old World Expo terrain.

Another one is Aquópolis, which is located outside the city center, in Sevilla Este. You can take a bus there and spend the day in a big pool complex with fun water slides. This is great if you're traveling with kids, or just love water slides.

There are also a few buses that will take you to the nearest beach in 1,5 hours. You can go to Matalascañas or Cádiz and make a day of it. If you're in Seville for a longer period, this might be a nice day trip to cool off a bit.

43. HORSE-DRAWN CARRIAGES IN SEVILLE

You see them everywhere in Seville, the typical horse-drawn carriages with their big yellow wheels and beautiful Andalusian horses in front of them. Did you know that the Moors used to go up the Giralda tower on horseback or in a small carriage behind their horse? Since they had to go up the tower 5 times a day, they were too lazy to walk up the stairs every time so instead they built a slope on the inside to make it easier for horses to carry them up to the top! Because of this tradition, you still see many horse-drawn carriages on the streets today.

The horses are very well taken care of. They do not work more than a few hours a day, they are all regularly checked and there are several 'horse stations' in the city where the horses can drink water and rest in the shade for a while.

You can go on a ride in one of these carriages. A ride takes about 45 minutes, and costs around €35. Beware, because during the Feria and Semana Santa, prices go up to €95 per ride. You can ask the coachman about the prices for a certain route. However, not all of them speak English. Some do

have audio tours available, so ask for more
information before you get in the carriage.

44. BUYING GROCERIES AND LITTLE THINGS

Of course, Seville has its supermarkets like any
other city in Spain. The Mercadona, Día, Supersol
and so on. There is also another type of shop that you
see everywhere in the city; the Chinese shop, or so
called 'Chino'. These are not just your ordinary
grocery shops. They have everything. From drinks, to
shoes, to gardening supplies. Anything you could
possibly need, you'll find there. They are usually tiny
shops with some typical souvenirs behind the
window. These tiny shops may not look like much
from the outside, but they really have everything you
need at a very low price.

If you're looking for something and you're not
having any luck at other shops, try the chinos.
Because if the chinos don't have it, it doesn't exist.

45. WATER FROM THE TAP

Don't worry, Sevillian water from the tap is perfectly safe and drinkable, but it might not taste the same as the water at home. This is because Andalusia is a very dry region that is more like a desert during the summer months. Therefore, the water must come from somewhere else, and there is a lot more that needs to be done to this water to make it drinkable. It also has something to do with the type of plumbing of the house you're staying in. If it has older copper pipes, it can change the taste of the water. This is why the water can sometimes taste bad, when you drink it directly from the tap.

There is something that you can do if you want fresh, cooler water that doesn't taste that bad. Let the water run for a few seconds before holding your glass underneath, the water will be a bit fresher and taste better.

46. NO SANGRIA?!

When you're in Spain, you'll have to drink sangria
at least once. At least. But what most tourists don't
know is that bars and restaurants do not have sangria
all year long. Most locals never drink sangria. They
call it the 'tourist-drink'. Sevillians opt for Tinto de
Verano – 'Summer Wine'. This is red wine, mixed
with Sprite or Fanta Lemon. Very easy to recreate,
this is one of the most popular drinks in Seville.
Especially during the summertime, this is what most
locals drink.

47. SOCCER IN SEVILLE

There are two soccer teams in Seville. Soccer is
the most popular sport in Spain, and Seville has the
biggest derby of the country. Sevilla F.C. has its
stadium in the Nervion district. Real Betis Balompié
has its stadium in Heliopolis. Both teams won the
Spanish National League and play at the same level.
There is a big rivalry between the fans of the two
teams, and every time Sevilla F.C. plays against Real
Betis, the whole city is either at the stadium, or glued

to their tv's. It is one of the most popular derbies in Spain.

You can visit both stadiums. The Real Betis stadium, called Benito Villamarin, is the 5th largest soccer stadium in Spain. It was recently renovated and it's open to the public. If you want to visit the stadiums, you can book a tour of the stadium, or go to a soccer match!

48. OLD ARCHIVES CAN BE QUITE INTERESTING

One of Seville's UNESCO World Heritage Sites is the Archivo de Indias. This beautiful building is located right in between the two other UNESCO World Heritage Sites in Seville, the Real Alcazar and the Cathedral. This archive used to be a market building for over 325 years, until the king of Spain decided that this was the perfect place to keep all the important documents created by the explorers of the 'New World' (of whom Cristopher Columbus is most noteworthy).

There is usually no line outside the archive, so you can walk right in. Among the more than 40.000

documents kept here you'll find a diary of Columbus,
a diary of famous Spanish writer Cervantes and a first
draft of Don Quixote, written by Cervantes. You'll
also find an old canon that used to be on a Spanish
ship that sunk just off the coast of Florida in the 16th
century. The ship was found in the 1990's, and its two
canons were still intact. One of these canons was kept
in Florida, and the other one was gifted by the
governor of Florida to the king of Spain, who then put
it on display in the Archivo de Indias in Seville.

If you're looking to kill some time in between
visiting the cathedral and you're interested in the
history of America, this is a great place to look
around!

49. MUSIC & CONCERTS

As I said before, Seville is the beating heart of
Flamenco music, but the city has so much more music
to offer. For example, La Alameda de Hércules is
where you'll find a big rock/punk/metal scene. There
are a few smaller concert halls/venues where bands
play every weekend.

If you'd like to visit a big open-air concert, you can go to the Auditorio Rocío Jurado. This auditorium was built for the World Expo of 1992, and it is still in use. The stage in this auditorium is one of the biggest stages in the world, and many different types of artists take the stage almost every weekend. There is something for everyone.

50. MUSEUM

Seville's old houses and museums have great art collections. I have mentioned a few already, but there is one more that is most definitely worth a visit, if you appreciate art, that is. The Museo de Bellas Artes in This museum was founded mid-nineteenth century in a 16th century building, and it houses a collection of paintings from the medieval period up to the 19th-20th century. Most of the collection is by Spanish, Flemish and Dutch masters. One of these Spanish masters is Bartolomé Murillo, a famous 17th century painter who was born and raised in Seville. He is Seville's pride and joy, and you'll see/hear his name often on the streets of Seville. For example, the Jardines de Murillo were named after him.

What makes this museum so interesting to me, is that the paintings give you a glimpse in to the Seville and Spain of 400 years ago. Some paintings show buildings that still stand today, but in a completely different scenery. They are not just beautiful paintings, they are a window into the past.

TOP REASONS TO BOOK THIS TRIP

History and culture as far as the eye can reach: Europe's largest historical center with its 3,000 years of history is paradise for history lovers.

The best tapas in Spain: Seville is Spain's culinary capital. Need I say more?

Convivial atmosphere all around: Days are long and nights even longer, streets always lively, buzzing with people and flamenco around every corner.

BONUS BOOK

50 THINGS TO KNOW ABOUT PACKING LIGHT FOR TRAVEL

PACK THE RIGHT WAY EVERY TIME

AUTHOR: MANIDIPA BHATTACHARYYA

Edited by Melanie Howthorne

ABOUT THE AUTHOR

Manidipa Bhattacharyya is a creative writer and editor, with an education in English literature and Linguistics. After working in the IT industry for seven long years she decided to call it quits and follow her heart instead. Manidipa has been ghost writing, editing, proof reading and doing secondary research services for many story tellers and article writers for about three years. She stays in Kolkata, India with her husband and a busy two year old. In her own time Manidipa enjoys travelling, photography and writing flash fiction.

Manidipa believes in travelling light and never carries anything that she couldn't haul herself on a trip. However, travelling with her child changed the scenario. She seemed to carry the entire world with her for the baby on the first two trips. But good sense prevailed and she is again working her way to becoming a light traveler, this time with a kid.

INTRODUCTION

He who would travel happily
must travel light.

-Antoine de Saint-Exupéry

Travel takes you to different places from seas and mountains to deserts and much more. In your travels you get to interact with different people and their cultures. You will, however, enjoy the sights and interact positively with these new people even more, if you are travelling light.

When you travel light your mind can be free from worry about your belongings. You do not have to spend precious vacation time waiting for your luggage to arrive after a long flight. There is be no chance of your bags going missing and the best part is that you need not pay a fee for checked baggage.

People who have mastered this art of packing light will root for you to take only one carry-on, wherever you go. However, many people can find it really hard to pack light. More so if you are travelling with children. Differentiating between "must have" and "just in case" items is the starting point. There will be ample shopping avenues at your destination which are just waiting to be explored.

This book will show you 'packing' in a new 'light' – pun intended – and help you to embrace light packing practices for all of your future travels.

Off to packing!

DEDICATION

I dedicate this book to all the travel buffs that I know, who have given me great insights into the contents of their backpacks.

THE RIGHT TRAVEL GEAR

1. CHOOSE YOUR TRAVEL GEAR CAREFULLY

While selecting your travel gear, pick items that are light weight, durable and most importantly, easy to carry. There are cases with wheels so you can drag them along – these are usually on the heavy side because of the trolley. Alternatively a backpack that you can carry comfortably on your back, or even a duffel bag that you can carry easily by hand or sling across your body are also great options. Whatever you choose, one thing to keep in mind is that the luggage itself should not weigh a ton, this will give you the flexibility to bring along one extra pair of shoes if you so desire.

2. CARRY THE MINIMUM NUMBER OF BAGS

Selecting light weight luggage is not everything. You need to restrict the number of bags you carry as well. One carry-on size bag is ideal for light travel. Most carriers allow one cabin baggage plus one purse, handbag or camera bag as long as it slides under the seat in front. So technically, you can carry two items of luggage without checking them in.

3. PACK ONE EXTRA BAG

Always pack one extra empty bag along with your essential items. This could be a very light weight duffel bag or even a sturdy tote bag which takes up minimal space. In the event that you end up buying a lot of souvenirs, you already have a handy bag to stuff all that into and do not have to spend time hunting for an appropriate bag.

I'm very strict with my packing and have everything in its right place. I never change a rule. I hardly use anything in the hotel room. I wheel my own wardrobe in and that's it.

Charlie Watts

CLOTHES & ACCESSORIES

4. PLAN AHEAD

Figure out in advance what you plan to do on your trip. That will help you to pick that one dress you need for the occasion. If you are going to attend a wedding then you have to carry formal wear. If not, you can ditch the gown for something lighter that will be comfortable during long walks or on the beach.

5. WEAR THAT JACKET

Remember that wearing items will not add extra luggage for your air travel. So wear that bulky jacket that you plan to carry for your trip. This saves space and can also help keep you warm during the chilly flight.

6. MIX AND MATCH

Carry clothes that can be interchangeably used to reinvent your look. Find one top that goes well with a couple of pairs of pants or skirts. Use tops, shirts and jackets wisely along with other accessories like a scarf or a stole to create a new look.

7. CHOOSE YOUR FABRIC WISELY

Stuffing clothes in cramped bags definitely takes its toll which results in wrinkles. It is best to carry wrinkle free, synthetic clothes or merino tops. This will eliminate the need for that small iron you usually bring along.

8. DITCH CLOTHES PACK UNDERWEAR

Pack more underwear and socks. These are the things that will give you a fresh feel even if you do not get a chance to wear fresh clothes. Moreover these are easy to wash and can be dried inside the hotel room itself.

9. CHOOSE DARK OVER LIGHT

While picking your clothes choose dark coloured ones. They are easy to colour coordinate and can last longer before needing a wash. Accidental food spills and dirt from the road are less visible on darker clothes.

10. WEAR YOUR JEANS

Take only one pair of Jeans with you, which you should wear on the flight. Remember to pick a pair that can be worn for sightseeing trips and is equally eloquent for dinner. You can add variety by adding light weight cargoes and chinos.

11. CARRY SMART ACCESSORIES

The right accessory can give you a fresh look even with the same old dress. An intelligent neck-piece, a couple of bright scarves, stoles or a sarong can be used in a number of ways to add variety to your clothing. These light weight beauties can double up as a nursing cover, a light blanket, beach wear, a modesty cover for visiting places of worship, and also makes for an enthralling game of peek-a-boo.

12. LEARN TO FOLD YOUR GARMENTS

Seasoned travellers all swear by rolling their clothes for compact and wrinkle free packing. Bundle packing, where you roll the clothes around a central object as if tying it up, is also a popular method of compact and wrinkle free packing. Stacking folded clothes one on top of another is a big no-no as it makes creases extreme and they are difficult to get rid of without ironing.

13. WASH YOUR DIRTY LAUNDRY

One of the ways to avoid carrying loads of clothes is to wash the clothes you carry. At some places you might get to use the laundry services or a Laundromat but if you are in a pinch, best solution is to wash them yourself. If that is the plan then carrying quick drying clothes is highly recommended, which most often also happen to be the wrinkle free variety.

14. LEAVE THOSE TOWELS BEHIND

Regular towels take up a lot of space, are heavy and take ages to dry out. If you are staying at hotels they will provide you with towels anyway. If you are travelling to a remote place, where the availability of towels look doubtful, carry a light weight travel towel of viscose material to do the job.

15. USE A COMPRESSION BAG

Compression bags are getting lots of recommendation now days from regular travellers. These are useful for saving space in your luggage when you have to pack bulky dresses. While packing for the return trip, get help from the hotel staff to arrange a vacuum cleaner.

FOOTWEAR

16. PUT ON YOUR HIKING BOOTS

If you have plans to go hiking or trekking during your trip, you will need those bulky hiking boots. The best way to carry them is to wear them on flight to save space and luggage weight. You can remove the boots once inside and be comfortable in your socks.

17. PICKING THE RIGHT SHOES

Shoes are often the bulkiest items, along with being the dainty if you are a female. They need care and take up a lot of space in your luggage. It is advisable therefore to pick shoes very carefully. If you plan to do a lot of walking and site seeing, then wearing a pair of comfortable walking shoes are a must. For more formal occasions you can carry durable, light weight flats which will not take up much space.

18. STUFF SHOES

If you happen to pack a pair of shoes, ensure you utilize their hollow insides. Tuck small items like rolled up socks or belts to save space. They will also be easy to find.

TOILETRIES

19. STASHING TOILETRIES

Carry only absolute necessities. Airline rules dictate
that for one carry-on bag, liquids and gels must be in
3.4 ounce (100ml) bottles or less, and must be packed
in a one quart zip-lock bag. If you are planning to stay
in a hotel, the basic things will be provided for you.
It's best is to buy the rest from the local market at
your destination.

20. TAKE ALONG TAMPONS

Tampons are a hard to find item in a lot of countries.
Figure out how many you need and pack accordingly.
For longer stays you can buy them online and have
them delivered to where you are staying.

21. GET PAMPERED BEFORE
YOU TRAVEL

Some avid travellers suggest getting a pedicure and
manicure just the day before travelling. This not only
gives you a well kept look, you also save the trouble
of packing nail polish. Remember, every little bit of
weight reduced adds up.

ELECTRONICS

22. LUGGING ALONG ELECTRONICS

Electronics have a large role to play in our lives today. Most of us cannot imagine our lives away from our phones, laptops or tablets. However while travelling, one must consider the amount of weight these electronics add to our luggage. Thankfully smart phones come along with all the essentials tools like a camera, email access, picture editing tools and more. They are smart to the point of eliminating the need to carry multiple gadgets. Choose a smart phone that suits all your requirements and travel with the world in your palms or pocket.

23. REDUCE THE NUMBER OF CHARGERS

If you do travel with multiple electronic devices, you will have to bear the additional burden of carrying all their chargers too. Check if a single charger can be used for multiple devices. You might also consider investing in a pocket charger. These small devices support multiple devices while keeping you charged on the go.

24. TRAVEL FRIENDLY APPS

Along with smart phones come numerous apps, which are immensely helpful in our travels. You name it and you have an app for it at hand – take pictures, sharing with friends and family, torch to light dark roads, maps, checking flight/train times, find hotels and many other things. Use these smart alternatives to traditional items like books to eliminate weight and save space.

I get ideas about what's essential when packing my suitcase.

-Diane von Furstenberg

TRAVELLING WITH KIDS

25. BRING ALONG THE STROLLER

Kids might enjoy walking for a while but they soon tire out and a stroller is the just the right thing for them to rest in while you continue your tour. Strollers also double duty as a luggage carrier and shopping bag holder. Remember to pick a light weight, easy to handle brand of stroller. Better yet, find out in advance if you can rent a stroller at your destination.

26. BRING ONLY ENOUGH DIAPERS FOR YOUR TRIP

Diapers take up a lot of space and add to the weight of your luggage. Therefore it is advisable to carry just enough diapers to last through the trip and a few for afterwards, till you buy fresh stock at your destination. Unless of course you are travelling to a really remote area, in which case you have no choice but to carry the load. Otherwise diapers are something you will find pretty easily.

27. TAKE ONLY A COUPLE OF TOYS

Children are easily attracted by new things in their environment. While travelling they will find numerous 'new' objects to scrutinize and play with. Packing just one favorite toy is enough, or if there is no favorite toy leave out all of them in favor of stories or imaginary games.

28. CARRY KID FRIENDLY SNACKS

Create a small snack counter in your bag to store away quick bites for those sudden hunger pangs. Depending on the child's age this could include chocolates, raisins, dry fruits, granola bars or biscuits. Also keep a bottle of water handy for your little one.

These things do not add much weight and can be adjusted in a handbag or knapsack.

29. GAMES TO CARRY

Create some travel specific, imaginary games if you have slightly grown up children, like spot the attractions. Keep a coloring book and colors handy for in-flight or hotel time. Apps on your smart phone can keep the children engaged with cartoons and story books. Older children are often entertained by games available on phones or tablets. This cuts the weight of luggage down while keeping the kids entertained.

30. LET THE KIDS CARRY THEIR LOAD

A good thing is to start early sharing of responsibilities. Let your child pick a bag of his or her choice and pack it themselves. Keep tabs on what they are stuffing in their bags by asking if they will be using that item on the trip. It could start out being just an entertainment bag initially but with growing years they will learn to sort the useful from the superfluous. Children as little as four can maneuver a small trolley suitcase like a pro- their experience in pull along toys credit. If you are worried that you may be pulling it for them, you may want to start with a backpack.

31. DECIDE ON LOCATION FOR CHILDREN TO SLEEP

While on a trip you might not always get a crib at your destination, and carrying one will make life all the more difficult. Instead call ahead to see if there are any cribs or roll out beds for children. You may even put blankets on the floor. Weave them a story about camping and they will gladly sleep without any trouble.

32. GET BABY PRODUCTS DELIVERED AT YOUR DESTINATION

If you are absolutely paranoid about not getting your favourite variety of diaper or brand of baby food, check out online stores like amazon.com for services in your destination city. You can buy things online ahead of your travel and get them delivered to your hotel upon arrival.

33. FEEDING NEEDS OF YOUR INFANTS

If you are travelling with a breastfed infant, you save the trouble of carrying bottles and bottle sanitization kits. For special food, or medications, you may need to call ahead to make sure you have a refrigerator where you are staying.

34. FEEDING NEEDS OF YOUR TODDLER

With the progression from infancy to toddler, their dietary requirements too evolve. You will have to pack some snacks for travelling time. Fresh fruits and vegetables can be purchased at your destination. Most of the cities you travel to in whichever part of the world, will have baby food products and formulas, available at the local drug-store or the supermarket.

35. PICKING CLOTHES FOR YOUR BABY

Contrary to popular belief, babies can do without many changes of clothes. At the most pack 2 outfits per day. Pack mix and match type clothes for your little one as well. Pick things which are comfortable to wear and quick to dry.

36. SELECTING SHOES FOR YOUR BABY

Like outfits, kids can make do with two pairs of comfortable shoes. If you can get some water resistant shoes it will be best. To expedite drying wet shoes, you can stuff newspaper in them then wrap

85

them with newspaper and leave them to dry
overnight.

37. KEEP ONE CHANGE OF CLOTHES HANDY

Travelling with kids can be tricky. Keep a change of
clothes for the kids and mum handy in your purse or
tote bag. This takes a bit of space in your hand
luggage but comes extremely handy in case there are
any accidents or spills.

38. LEAVE BEHIND BABY ACCESSORIES

Baby accessories like their bed, bath tub, car seat, crib
etc. should be left at home. Many hotels provide a
crib on request, while car seats can be borrowed from
friends or rented. Babies can be given a bath in the
hotel sink or even in the adult bath tub with a little bit
of water. If you bring a few bath toys, they can be
used in the bath, pool, and out of water. They can also
be sanitized easily in the sink.

39. CARRY A SMALL LOAD OF PLASTIC BAGS

With children around there are chances of a number
of soiled clothes and diapers. These plastic bags help
to sort the dirt from the clean inside your big bag.

These are very light weight and come in handy to other carry stuff as well at times.

PACK WITH A PURPOSE

40. PACKING FOR BUSINESS TRIPS

One neutral-colored suit should suffice. It can be paired with different shirts, ties and accessories for different occasions. One pair of black suit pants could be worn with a matching jacket for the office or with a snazzy top for dinner.

41. PACKING FOR A CRUISE

Most cruises have formal dinners, and that formal dress usually takes up a lot of space. However you might find a tuxedo to rent. For women, a short black dress with multiple accessory options will do the trick.

42. PACKING FOR A LONG TRIP OVER DIFFERENT CLIMATES

The secret packing mantra for travel over multiple climates is layering. Layering traps air around your body creating insulation against the cold. The same light t-shirt that is comfortable in a warmer climate can be the innermost layer in a colder climate.

REDUCE SOME MORE WEIGHT

43. LEAVE PRECIOUS THINGS AT HOME

Things that you would hate to lose or get damaged leave them at home. Precious jewelry, expensive gadgets or dresses, could be anything. You will not require these on your trip. Leave them at home and spare the load on your mind.

44. SEND SOUVENIRS BY MAIL

If you have spent all your money on purchasing souvenirs, carrying them back in the same bag that you brought along would be difficult. Either pack everything in another bag and check it in the airport or get everything shipped to your home. Use an international carrier for a secure transit, but this could be more expensive than the checking fees at the airport.

45. AVOID CARRYING BOOKS

Books equal to weight. There are many reading apps which you can download on your smart phone or tab.

Plus there are gadgets like Kindle and Nook that are thinner and lighter alternatives to your regular book.

CHECK, GET, SET, CHECK AGAIN

46. STRATEGIZE BEFORE PACKING

Create a travel list and prepare all that you think you need to carry along. Keep everything on your bed or floor before packing and then think through once again – do I really need that? Any item that meets this question can be avoided. Remove whatever you don't really need and pack the rest.

47. TEST YOUR LUGGAGE

Once you have fully packed for the trip take a test trip with your luggage. Take your bags and go to town for window shopping for an hour. If you enjoy your hour long trip it is good to go, if not, go home and reduce the load some more. Repeat this test till you hit the right weight.

48. ADD A ROLL OF DUCT TAPE

You might wonder why, when this book has been talking about reducing stuff, we're suddenly asking you to pack something totally unusual. This is because when you have limited supplies, duct tape is immensely helpful for small repairs – a broken bag, leaking zip-lock bag, broken sunglasses, you name it and duct tape can fix it, temporarily.

49. LIST OF ESSENTIAL ITEMS

Even though the emphasis is on packing light, there are things which have to be carried for any trip. Here is our list of essentials:

• Passport/Visa or any other ID

• Any other paper work that might be required on a trip like permits, hotel reservation confirmations etc.

• Medicines – all your prescription medicines and emergency kit, especially if you are travelling with children

• Medical or vaccination records

• Money in foreign currency if travelling to a different country

• Tickets- Email or Message them to your phone

50. MAKE THE MOST OF YOUR TRIP

Wherever you are going, whatever you hope to do we encourage you to embrace it whole-heartedly. Take in the scenery, the culture and above all, enjoy your time away from home.

On a long journey even a straw weighs heavy.

-Spanish Proverb

PACKING AND PLANNING TIPS

A Week before Leaving

- Arrange for someone to take care of pets and water plants.

- Stop mail and newspaper.

- Notify Credit Card companies where you are going.

- Change your thermostat settings.

- Car inspected, oil is changed, and tires have the correct pressure.

- Passports and photo identification is up to date.

- Pay bills.

- Copy important items and download travel Apps.

- Start collecting small bills for tips.

Right Before Leaving

- Clean out refrigerator.

- Empty garbage cans.

- Lock windows.

- Make sure you have the proper identification with you.

- Bring cash for tips.

- Remember travel documents.

- Lock door behind you.

- Remember wallet.

- Unplug items in house and pack chargers.

>TOURIST

READ OTHER
GREATER THAN A TOURIST
BOOKS

Greater Than a Tourist San Miguel de Allende Guanajuato Mexico:
50 Travel Tips from a Local by Tom Peterson

Greater Than a Tourist – Lake George Area New York USA:
50 Travel Tips from a Local by Janine Hirschklau

Greater Than a Tourist – Monterey California United States:
50 Travel Tips from a Local by Katie Begley

Greater Than a Tourist – Chanai Crete Greece:
50 Travel Tips from a Local by Dimitra Papagrigoraki

Greater Than a Tourist – The Garden Route Western Cape Province
South Africa: 50 Travel Tips from a Local by Li-Anne McGregor van
Aardt

Greater Than a Tourist – Sevilla Andalusia Spain:
50 Travel Tips from a Local by Gabi Gazon

Greater Than a Tourist – Kota Bharu Kelantan Malaysia:
50 Travel Tips from a Local by Aditi Shukla

Children's Book: Charlie the Cavalier Travels the World by Lisa
Rusczyk

>TOURIST

> TOURIST

Visit Greater Than a Tourist for Free Travel Tips
http://GreaterThanATourist.com

Sign up for the Greater Than a Tourist Newsletter for
discount days, new books, and travel information:
http://eepurl.com/cxspyf

Follow us on Facebook for tips, images, and ideas:
https://www.facebook.com/GreaterThanATourist

Follow us on Pinterest for travel tips and ideas:
http://pinterest.com/GreaterThanATourist

Follow us on Instagram for beautiful travel images:
http://Instagram.com/GreaterThanATourist

>TOURIST

> TOURIST

Please leave your honest review of this book on Amazon and Goodreads. Please send your feedback to GreaterThanaTourist@gmail.com as we continue to improve the series. We appreciate your positive and constructive feedback. Thank you.

METRIC CONVERSIONS

TEMPERATURE

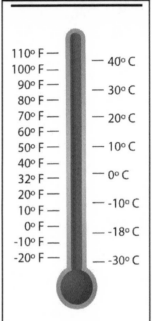

110° F — — 40° C
100° F —
90° F — — 30° C
80° F —
70° F — — 20° C
60° F —
50° F — — 10° C
40° F —
32° F — — 0° C
20° F —
10° F — — -10° C
0° F —
-10° F — — -18° C
-20° F — — -30° C

To convert F to C:

Subtract 32, and then multiply by 5/9 or .5555.

To Convert C to F:

Multiply by 1.8 and then add 32.

32F = 0C

LIQUID VOLUME

To Convert:.................Multiply by
U.S. Gallons to Liters................. 3.8
U.S. Liters to Gallons 26
Imperial Gallons to U.S. Gallons 1.2
Imperial Gallons to Liters....... 4.55
Liters to Imperial Gallons 22
1 Liter = .26 U.S. Gallon
1 U.S. Gallon = 3.8 Liters

DISTANCE

To convert ....Multiply by
Inches to Centimeters 2.54
Centimeters to Inches 39
Feet to Meters...................... .3
Meters to Feet 3.28
Yards to Meters 91
Meters to Yards 1.09
Miles to Kilometers 1.61
Kilometers to Miles............. .62
1 Mile = 1.6 km
1 km = .62 Miles

WEIGHT

1 Ounce = .28 Grams
1 Pound = .4555 Kilograms
1 Gram = .04 Ounce
1 Kilogram = 2.2 Pounds

TRAVEL QUESTIONS

- Do you bring presents home to family or friends after a vacation?

- Do you get motion sick?

- Do you have a favorite billboard?

- Do you know what to do if there is a flat tire?

- Do you like a sun roof open?

- Do you like to eat in the car?

- Do you like to wear sun glasses in the car?

- Do you like toppings on your ice cream?

- Do you use public bathrooms?

- Did you bring your cell phone and does it have power?

- Do you have a form of identification with you?

- Have you ever been pulled over by a cop?

- Have you ever given money to a stranger on a road trip?

- Have you ever taken a road trip with animals?

- Have you ever went on a vacation alone?

- Have you ever run out of gas?

- If you could move to any place in the world, where would it be?

- If you could travel anywhere in the world, where would you travel?

- If you could travel in any vehicle, which one would it be?

- If you had three things to wish for from a magic genie, what would they be?

- If you have a driver's license, how many times did it take you to pass the test?

- What are you the most afraid of on vacation?

- What do you want to get away from the most when you are on vacation?

- What foods smells bad to you?

- What item do you bring on ever trip with you away from home?

- What makes you sleepy?

- What song would you love to hear on the radio when you're cruising on the highway?

- What travel job would you want the least?

- What will you miss most while you are away from home?

- What is something you always wanted to try?

- What is the best road side attraction that you ever saw?

- What is the farthest distance you ever biked?

- What is the farthest distance you ever walked?

- What is the weirdest thing you needed to buy while on vacation?

- What is your favorite candy?

- What is your favorite color car?

- What is your favorite family vacation?

- What is your favorite food?

- What is your favorite gas station drink or food?

- What is your favorite license plate design?

- What is your favorite restaurant?

- What is your favorite smell?

- What is your favorite song?

- What is your favorite sound that nature makes?

- What is your favorite thing to bring home from a vacation?

- What is your favorite vacation with friends?

- What is your favorite way to relax?

105

- Where is the farthest place you ever traveled in a car?

- Where is the farthest place you ever went North, South, East and West?

- Where is your favorite place in the world?

- Who is your favorite singer?

- Who taught you how to drive?

- Who will you miss the most while you are away?

- Who if the first person you will contact when you get to your destination?

- Who brought you on your first vacation?

- Who likes to travel the most in your life?

- Would you rather be hot or cold?

- Would you rather drive above, below, or at the speed limited?

- Would you rather drive on a highway or a back road?

- Would you rather go on a train or a boat?

- Would you rather go to the beach or the woods?

TRAVEL BUCKET LIST

1.

2.

3.

4.

5.

6.

7.

8.

9.

10.